MOMENTS OF GRATITUDE

MOMENTS OF GRATITUDE

Christine McNamara

First published in Australia in 2017 by Christine McNamara

Copyright © Christine McNamara 2017

Email: momentsofgratitude2017@gmail.com
Website: www.momentsofgratitude.com.au

The moral right of the author has been asserted.

All rights reserved.
No part of this publication may be reproduced, stored in a retrieval system or transmitted in any form or by any means without the prior permission of the publisher, nor be otherwise circulated in any form of binding or cover other than that in which it is published.

National Library of Australia Cataloguing-in-Publication entry:

Creator   McNamara, Christine – author

Title   Moments of Gratitude / by Christine McNamara

ISBN   9780648100713 (paperback)

Subjects   Australian poetry.
          Life – Poetry.
          Gratitude – Poetry.

To share my sense of adventure and have an
extraordinary happy life.

Contents

Infinite Circles	1
At Least I Am Alive	2
Happy Valentine's Day	3
Love to All	4
Enchanted Love	5
Be Yourself	6
Moment of Magic	7
Mirror	8
Love	9
Lost in our Space	10
The Twins Wrestle	11
The Meaning of Life	12
A Healing Connection	13
You Are With Me	14
I Want More	15
A Calling of Love	16
Respect	17
Thoughts So Far Today	18
Dear God	19
Romance	20
Giving	21
Attraction	22
The Adventure of Life	23
The Contrasts of Life	24

Reunion	25
La Catte	26
Reflections	27
Not Knowing	28
Sheer Joy	29
Date with Destiny	31
Happiness is a Choice	32
Restlessness of the Soul	33
Blessed Reunion	34
A New Dance	35
Possibilities	36
Free to be Me	37
Angels Everywhere	38
World of Bliss	39
Money	40
The Unexpected	41
Change	42
Heartbeat	43
Everything is Easy	44
Know What You Want	45
How Do You Know?	46
The Freedom to be Me	47
Burning the Past	48
I Love You	49
My Love	50
Moment to Moment	51
About the Author	53

Infinite Circles

It's funny this feeling that I have inside
It is beautiful, so beautiful and also very real
By breaking down the barriers I feel so warm
It is special
How wonderful it is to be alive and free of inhibition

There have been many magic moments in my life
and there are many more to come
Gratitude for one's blessings and challenges to greet
With passion for your dreams
You can grow and

'round the circle goes!

Christine McNamara

At Least I Am Alive

I feel confused, dissatisfied with my lot
Can't understand this feeling of disinterest and self destruction
Overwhelmed and hardest on myself
It's a pattern that I don't want
I look for reasons, I analyse, I get frustrated
there's no quick-fix solution at hand

I have everything that I want
I have chosen this path

At times, being accountable *just* stinks

When I feel out of control and spiralling down
I suppose one should finish with ...
At least I am alive!

Happy Valentine's Day

My gorgeous man
each morning when I walk I think of you
You are my dream come true
You are everything I want in a man

I admire you for your honesty with me
And I respect what you teach me
What we share is a gift
What we desire is ours to enjoy

Be my Valentine … love always!

Christine McNamara

Love to All

We spoke this morning and yet –
it seems a life-time away
I want to call him again
just to hear what he wants to say
When we speak, I feel him
He has become a part of me

I have been looking at our differences
and judging the inadequacies
Clearly I must change this vision
as really we have a synergy

I must love myself first, the rest will follow
as love begets love in God's world
I am grateful for the gift that I have
and for the people that I share it with

To love myself is to love all

Enchanted Love

I see the world through different eyes
and enjoy the journey often
So many dreams can come true
when you be –
instead of do
I plan to bring enchanted love into my life
and create a grand and adventurous future
Fill it with joy and celebrate often

Smell the roses
Gratitude is cleansing
I am prepared to receive him into my heart

And experience that enchanted love

Christine McNamara

Be Yourself

To begin with the end in mind
puts it all into perspective
you will find
Be who you are
be true to yourself
and the world outside, don't kid thyself

Billy Thorpe, you are an example for all
You lived your life true to yourself

Thank you for touching my life
and reminding me that
love is all that matters

Moment of Magic

To be who you are and be loved
What a wonderful feeling!
The magic to express yourself
and to be accepted

To be so open and have another witness you
experience the depths of connection
and be uplifted
To love and be loved is a state of magic

Stars shoot across the sky
like fireworks
The heavens open
The earth moves

Oh, to be human
It is beauty
but also
vulnerability …

Mirror

It is wonderful to be here with you
I realise how lucky I am to have someone
who cares so much
Your body is warm and inviting
I melt into your skin
To kiss you is a gift
I am grateful for these soft tender lips
that are so full of love

I celebrate my freedom
to choose who I am
and how I spend my life
I choose to spend this moment with you
You are my escape
my lifeline and my champion
I feel you even if you are not with me

How do I express the way I feel about you?
I guess the word is mirror

Love

When another touches your heart and soul
they understand who you are
and make you feel as if in that moment –
there is no one else but you

Christine McNamara

Lost in our Space

You are in my thoughts
You make my life rich with intense emotion
You turned on the lights and life is brighter
A constant string of happy moments

I am amazed by your desire to please me
You're giving of yourself; your total presence
I am grateful that I share this incredible space with you
There is no other like you
You are one in a million

The Twins Wrestle

I feel alive and wanted
To hear you say how much you miss me
and that you can't wait to see me
is to be on top of the world with happiness
This emotion completes the circle of my life
and it is all that I need
All that I can hope for is this sharing of moments
and to let go of what I cannot control

I know that I am going somewhere with you
To want to have a destination
To share the ups and downs
the magic, and the tragic
the adventure and the boredom
of growing old together watching movies
reading books and hanging out with friends
to create a history that is ours
Take each moment and cherish it as if it were the last

Give all that you feel and receive all that is given
To have you and feel like this every day
Is to be grateful for a life blessed with love, joy and time together

Christine McNamara

The Meaning of Life

To be free and choose how life should be
To feel good from the inside out
To know that you have a purpose
and are loved and guided
are keys that can unlock the meaning of life

But the true meaning to life is individual

And for me, it is to share my sense of adventure
and live an extraordinarily happy life.

A Healing Connection

I wish I could take his pain
make it all go away
I can see he is deeply challenged by it
but his strength will carry him through
I want to hug and hold him
but I know that he must walk this path alone
and that I am just a supporter along the way

A role I hold with deep respect
This man has held me close and exposed his soul totally

I feel incredibly touched beyond skin and intelligence
He has found my soul and warmed it with pure kindness
Bless this connection and what we share

Christine McNamara

You Are With Me

I think about crawling into bed next to you
and resting my head upon your chest
Feeling warm, safe, protected and loved

I miss you in my life
I miss the happiness; I miss the laughter
You were an incredible inspiration in my life
And seeing you was always a magic moment

I can still feel your presence
It means so much that you shared how you felt
I want you to know that I am a changed woman
for having shared your space

I Want More

I visualise our meeting
I imagine the first kiss
Knowing I will want more
than to just touch lips …

To be held in a hug
To hear your heart beat
and feel your breath
knowing I can barely breathe
from excitement

Champagne, chocolates
What will our indulgence be?
To hang out and feel more than
I will want to let go of

Just to anticipate these moments
makes me smile
And if this is all that life can give
then I shall be in heaven when I am with you

Christine McNamara

A Calling of Love

The time has come
I am ready to let go and move on
And the heart catches up with the head
I see the gift of love and happiness
A second chance to be free
In the arms of a man who deserves to be loved

I will relax and enjoy who I have become
I feel the desire to live each moment
and share an intimate communion with my soul
How lucky to have purpose
and a chance to be loved
Just as I am

Respect

A storm has been brewing
and the ocean is furious
I need to clear the decks and start afresh
My feelings are too intense and do not suit the situation
Things have gone too far
From this point on, I am in over my head

I am sad that I can go no further
But the facts are the facts
I don't really know why I cannot continue
The pressure is too much
No availability
I want more than is on offer
He decides and I may not like it but I respect it.

Christine McNamara

Thoughts So Far Today

The body wrapped in avocado
A foot massage that releases
all the tension this body has stored

The body rejuvenates
Time to sit, to doze and then awaken
to a beautiful view of the Peruvian coast
The misty outlook calms me and I feel as if
I am in a time warp

I taste delicious food that awakens my mouth
Hmm … three small chocolates and coffee

Dear God

I trust you with my life
Guide me on my path
May my life be filled with love and happiness
And all things be as they should be

When I doubt my path
remind me that my soul
is bigger than the universe
and that all is well

Show me guidance and help me
to be open to you
and to see my life through your eyes.

Christine McNamara

Romance

I am a hopeless romantic
and every moment of getting to know someone
is like watching a flower open
I hold my breath hearing everything they say
My warming heart
opening to the bloom of possibility

I feel excitement being with a friend
who makes me feel alive and special
Anticipating that at any moment
what is everyday could be spectacular, passionate
An intimate communion

Giving

To invest in love through effort
To want another to feel the time
the thought and kindness through a small gift
in hope they receive in the spirit of giving

One day I may be the receiver and I will
look back in fond memory

For now I get to spend the day
with a special friend doing special acts of kindness
and share a wonderful opportunity
This time is two magical things at once
A memory etched forever

Attraction

When I see you my body vibrates
You rock the very core of my existence
Your look, those eyes are the keys to secrets

It's as if you move in slow motion
I observe every muscle, every sinew
Your body is sculptured and firm yet soft to touch
Perfection …
I see the hunger for life
for the future
To conquer and be free

A reflection of me
A kiss, a touch, is there more?
Will the sparks ignite a passion that must be satisfied?

The Adventure of Life

I sometimes wonder about my life's twists and turns
It's like so many lives in one
I think of all the places I have lived
and those that I have visited
So many seasons, and so many moments

I dreamed of this life from very young
and it has been more than any dream could hold
The adventure of this life has had it all
like an epic film – almost scripted and not real
I like that I can fill my time with dreams of future moments

Christine McNamara

The Contrasts of Life

Escaping from the hustle and bustle
does wonders for the soul
I am grounded through family connection
and the depth of what this world has created
My roots are in the country
It is a synergy I cannot explain
other than a feeling of being just where I belong

The pure air and sky
make it so easy to relax and forget all
except these moments
These special and precious moments
that remind us of what life is about

It is a blessing to be present and grateful
for the green, for the blue
A reminder of the contrasts of life

Reunion

Our reunion was the re-igniting of the flame
A year gone by and the passion is deeper
The desire to love and give more
is now never ending

Escape to a fantasy world, a stark contrast
to the race run during the day
It is almost too good to be true
And then back to the real world

Reality bites …

A chance the fairytale may be burst with truth
and blow the lives of others lives apart
I feel the turmoil, the sadness and fear
as I open the door of no return

If only I could make it easier
But he must stand alone and decide
It's his future
May his strength and courage be at hand

Christine McNamara

La Catte

The time spent with friends and lovers
is magnificent to me
I live in these moments in awe
of the depth of feeling
I wonder if they can see

When I escape to my home
the peace I feel
is truly rejuvenating
It's time to be just me

I grow as I learn and experience life's adventures
in the quiet moments with books and journals
In the garden, the house and most importantly –
with Bruce the cat

Life is there to be savoured
one
day
at a time

Reflections

I wonder what a man sees when he looks into my eyes
What I see in theirs is innocence
A soul that yearns to be touched
I feel alive and passionate when I gaze into eyes wide open
held in a moment of connection beyond the touch
The more I am present in the moment
the easier it is to hold that moment
Beyond this time and space
Into the cells, the body stores an everlasting reminder of
how wonderful to be touched and connected forever

Christine McNamara

Not Knowing

Excitement!
To not know fully how another feels
The possibility of more
Or not
Maybe only the feeling
will go on without knowing

I have found a place of satisfaction
that requires no participation
Just the thoughts of what could be
the conscious moment
the knowing when a dream comes true

It is still just a string of moments across a lifetime
Maybe I am in a place where expectation no longer lives
The old has now been replaced by the new
The growth has taken place and my time has come

Synchronicity!
it all happens for a reason and in the right time
When I feel a warm blanket of love wrap around me
I know I have found a mate
with whom to share time and space

Sheer Joy

Another year ticks over and I feel at peace
I am in tune, relaxed, enjoying life
I have all that I wanted for myself at this time
Friendships, fun and a life that suits me

I feel quietly alive,
not a care in the world
A rhythm that is calming
No surprises.

The calm before the storm
maybe a good storm,
one of stirring and sparks
to light up the sky
The slumber before waking
the collecting of my thoughts
before opening and sharing

My love affair with God
has reached new heights
I now know that I am complete
able to conjure all that is necessary to be special

No one can do this quite like I can
and knowing I stand alone
to be who I am is liberating

Christine McNamara

Let me see where this new-found friendship will lead
Into my soul with sheer joy.

Date with Destiny

I have thought about this day for many months
It seemed so far away and a mountain to climb
But now it has arrived it is just like any other day

It makes me wonder about all the build up
Is it just a game I play
to keep me focused on the possibilities?

I realise it can only ever be as good
as the reality of the moment
I want to suspend some of these moments in time
because they are so high, so grand, so real
and touch another with all my passion

Christine McNamara

Happiness is a Choice

I know that when I open my heart
a light shines out and touches another
And if their heart is open the light joins
and for a brief moment in time the glow
illuminates the room

I feel alive; loved; connected, and complete
I return to my life and continue on
remembering a faint but raw image
And then I want more

I remind myself that life is all about contrasts
and that I am blessed with many grand moments
I am aware and feel it all
I feel joy within
and I express myself honestly
I make the choice to the happy.
I share my moments with wonderful friends
But I still want more

Satisfied – never; hungry, always

Restlessness of the Soul

An unsatisfied desire
A yearning deep within
To be loved – no strings
Just loved and cherished for being me

This unresolved desire leads
me down the path of no future
and the soul cannot break through
It is time to go deep and heal
To know there is no more searching
looking or desiring but an end
to the restlessness of the soul

Christine McNamara

Blessed Reunion

Passing time has made it clear
that our love is deep
true and real
Nothing will change it
It is what it is
Or, is it all too good to be true?

To live in his space and exist
within the impossible dream
Moments that light the flame
The release of months of tension
Too much to risk?

Trusting that these moments
are presented at just the right time
to give me what I need
I long to grow this new-found depth of soul
letting me be me

A New Dance

The dance begins
A chance meeting
The timing all out
An unsatisfied feeling
There must be more …

A sense of urgency
A drawing together of sharing
Opening and finding more
An excitement that
must be investigated …

Each moment leads to the next
building a stronger connection
Wanting to touch, kiss – is it real?
On the edge, wanting to fall in
The warm and stronger kiss desirable
Imagination runs wild with the possibility of more …

The music ends
Sit in this chair, relax, and enjoy
until the next dance begins

Possibilities

You sent me a vibe and I felt it!
Then off you went to explore your universe
It seemed so easy when you returned
to just pick up where we left off
You're changed and now open to let me in

The dance of connection has begun
and it is amazing to observe
I hear everything that you say
and all that you do brings more
energy to an all-encompassing moment
and I am sensitive to it all

We touch, we play, we laugh,
we make each moment come alive
You kissed me goodnight
and I fell into your world
So sweet, warm and unknown
Will you take me to where all is possible?

Free to be Me

To watch the ebb and flow of life
and grow and change
To accept what is before me
without expectation or understanding
To trust and be open
To experience and be happy
It is beautiful to watch a friendship blossom
and to be so present to laugh, cry
and be so supported and accepted

To tap into the energy and feel loved
And enjoy being free to be me

Angels Everywhere

To be so connected and aware
Is like magic in slow motion
Softness is power and
blessings are everywhere

So simple to let the universe provide
To kiss, laugh, play and be consumed
Submit and dominate without a care
There are angels everywhere

World of Bliss

A man comes to me when he cares
I feel him in every sense
His words go deep into my soul
and I want to remember him forever

It is a moment of greatness
A recognition of my existence
when I feel wanted
and encouraged to be more
I want to go forward
Look ahead
and create a world of bliss

Money

My relationship with money has been a lifelong struggle
to understand its power in the physical world
It comes and it goes
It sets the pace
It determines the geography

This problem awaits a miracle to solve it
but I forgo its control
I truly let go
I no longer need it to be happy

When it's not around I have
the freedom to choose a simple life
and take an easier path

The Unexpected

No comfort as I have known it before
Living a life that was unexpected
So many differences to what I dared dream
It truly is another life!

I face all my fears and it feels unreal
to be still standing in a world
that no longer spins the way that I thought
and I've stopped wondering why

I must believe in this path
All will unfold as it should
I will stay and summon the magic from within!

Christine McNamara

Change

To create the life I want
is to dream big and allow it to come to me
A change in one creates a change in all
bringing with it time
space and a feeling of the universe
having taken care of it all
Take a chance, take a leap

Close one door and open another on a whole new life
Move across the water and begin to relax, enjoy and release
Feel and be taken to bliss by letting love
trust and openness touch my heart

Heartbeat

I rest my head on your chest
and hear the beat of your heart
Fast, excited and into us
I'm thrilled that our lives have merged
and everything has changed in a heartbeat

We attracted each other to one
warm and loving
moment-to-moment embrace
And found our reflection in that place

My soul sees your soul
and as friendly, laughing and connected as we are
there is a deep understanding that what we have
is extraordinary and I treasure this space

Everything is Easy

We meet, and then we meet again
It's so simple to be with each other
Time flows and conversation is easy

How wonderful it is to be present
and know that this is perfect
Just allowing each other to be

Effortless and connected we are
free to fulfill our own desires and
brought together to nourish our souls

Know What You Want

To touch and learn what another wants, needs, desires
To allow another to be just as they are
flows back to you as love, care and concern

Give them their freedom and watch them grow stronger
and they return to you with renewed energy
and as fresh as if you have just met

Know what you want and then ask
so they can give you the pleasure
of being as free and wild –
the very best of who you can be

Christine McNamara

How Do You Know?

Deep within, a calling, a question
that sparks a conversation on a topic
that has never arisen before
The courage to put feelings on the line
to say how you truly feel

Clarity
Knowing the future
allows another to choose and respond
with equal courage and clarity

Simple, easy; over in a moment
Together from now on without question again
Acceptance that our journey together is now forever

The Freedom to be Me

Feeling free for the first time
can only be explained now
As a joy and knowing that I can have it all

Allowing the possibility
A thought that can become reality
Remembering that love awaits me
when my day is done

A beautiful awakening that I feel every time
I return from life's work
to rest in that moment
I celebrate there is more joy to share
Every day feels like the first
Two lives now intertwined

Burning the Past

The blood moon rose
and an opportunity blossomed
The call to burn
Make it happen

Stirring the embers one last time
knowing I have found my paradise
The lessons learned
The love lost
to define what I want

Here now is beyond my imagination
A truly happy moment
The lights go on
and my world brightens

I Love You

The instant I felt I loved you I told you
I watched you take it in and receive me
I am so happy and my life is full
of precious time with my man

I am taking all that life has to offer
I feel your passion and I want more
taking me to places
that are my greatest adventures

You truly care and are very tender
You melt my body and I let go
as pure happiness floods my existence
feeding the fire for more

Christine McNamara

My Love

It is in moments of clarity
that I write poetry
When the world slows down
and is measured moment to moment
Me, just being instead of doing

Learning the truth and being true to myself
I celebrate and deep in my soul
I feel happy, loved and treasured
by a man I love
The reality I choose
Starts in the morning, every morning

Moment to Moment

I am rested and as I emerge
I promise to live only in each moment
The thought in every moment
connecting me to who I am
as I create and love thoughtfully

I trust each moment
accepting it with gratitude
Being aware that as each moment passes
another appears, bringing fresh new thoughts
and experiences

About the Author

Christine McNamara is person who has been searching for a purpose and deeper meaning to life.

In this search she has dabbled in many different areas, always open to learn and grow.

Preferring to see life as more than just a string of random events, somewhere between creating your own world and having a predetermined destiny.

This book of poetry is a reflection of that journey.

www.ingramcontent.com/pod-product-compliance
Lightning Source LLC
LaVergne TN
LVHW051512070426
835507LV00022B/3067